101 FLUTE TIPS

STUFF ALL THE PROS KNOW AND USE

BY ELAINE SCHMIDT

On the demo CD:
Jennifer Clippert, flutist

We gratefully acknowledge the Muramatsu Flute Mfg. Co., Ltd.
for allowing us to photograph one of their flutes.

ISBN 978-1-4803-4543-0

HAL•LEONARD®
CORPORATION

7777 W. BLUEMOUND RD. P.O. BOX 13819 MILWAUKEE, WI 53213

In Australia Contact:
Hal Leonard Australia Pty. Ltd.
4 Lentara Court
Cheltenham, Victoria, 3192 Australia
Email: ausadmin@halleonard.com.au

Visit Hal Leonard Online at
www.halleonard.com

TABLE OF CONTENTS

1 GETTING ACQUAINTED WITH THE FLUTE – THE BIG PICTURE

Welcome to the longest instrumental tradition on the planet. The earliest musical instruments were simple flutes, some of which have been found to date back more than 40,000 years. Fortunately for us, our instrument has evolved from those early pieces of carved bone, to the silver, keyed instrument we know today.

Modern flutes break down into three major sections:

- The head joint creates the core sound of the instrument. Beginning flutists start out by making a simple "toot" sound on just the head joint of the instrument before assembling the flute.

- The body is the longest section of the flute and contains most of the instrument's key mechanism.

- The foot joint is the smallest section of the instrument.

Now that you can identify the flute and its various parts, take special note of the barrel. It is part of the body of the flute and it contains no keys or ribbing. The flute maker's name and the instrument's serial number are found here, but the barrel is more than a signboard. It makes the perfect spot to place your hand when you are holding or carrying a flute. If you grab or carry the flute with your hand clasped around the keys, you risk bending parts of the fragile key-and-ribbing system. If you carry it while holding onto just the head joint, you risk having the flute slide free of the head joint and hit the floor.

barrel

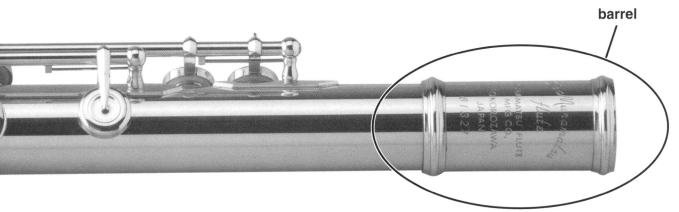

Keep the flute in front of you as you move around, holding it by the barrel with the head joint up, perpendicular to the floor. If you carry your flute this way, you have less chance of bumping it into doorframes, music stands, or other obstacles as you move about than if you are carrying to your side or parallel to the floor.

5

The head joint of the flute contains the lip plate and embouchure hole of the instrument.

The closed end of the head joint is capped by the crown, which turns to move the tuning cork that is located inside that end of the head joint. Look at Tip 55 for information on proper handling of the crown and cork.

The portion of the head joint that is inserted into the body of the flute is called the tenon, as is the part of the body that is inserted into the foot joint.

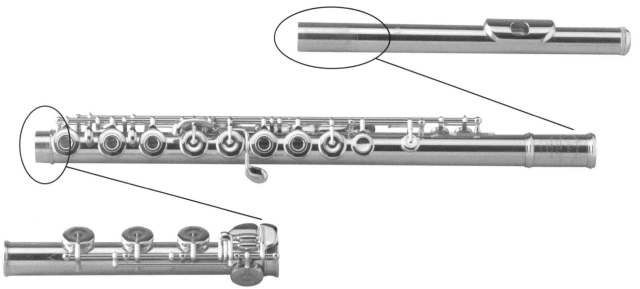

The long metal tubes that are connected to the keys are called ribs. The short posts that connect these ribs to the body of the flute are called just that: posts. The tiny metal bars hidden beneath the ribs are the springs that allow keys to pop open or return to a closed position when not in use.

The lowest note on a student flute is middle C. Step-up and professional flutes have an additional key on the foot joint that allows the flute to play a low B. The tiny button key on the footjoint, which allows the player to add just the low B key to high C to sweeten that note, is called the gizmo. No kidding, that's its name.

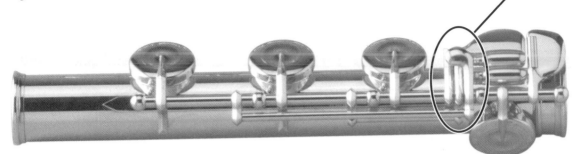

4 ASSEMBLING AND DISASSEMBLING YOUR FLUTE

The vast majority of damage that occurs to flutes can be prevented with a little attention to how the flute is handled. These few simple rules will help prevent bent and broken keys as well as a bent flute.

Always hold the body, as well as the assembled flute, by the barrel, never by the keys.

incorrect   **correct**

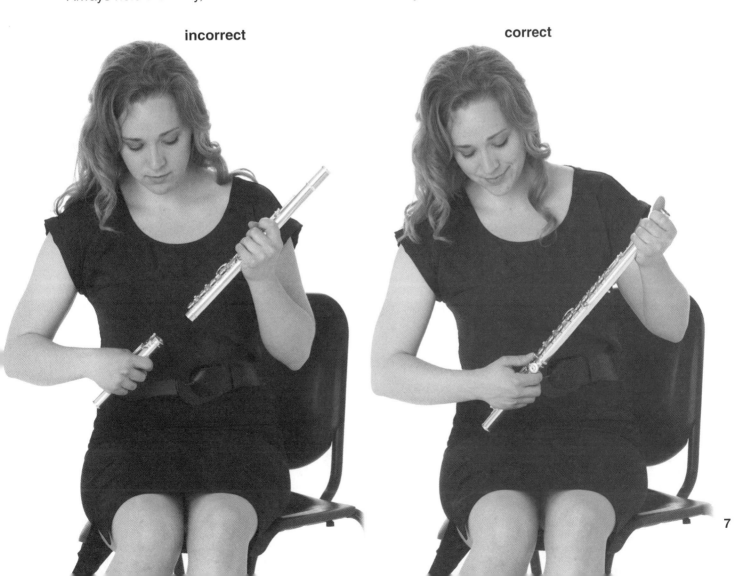

Holding the foot joint as pictured so that you are not gripping the keys, always twist the sections gently as you put the flute together.

Line up the embouchure hole with the key covered by your left-hand first finger. Line up the ribbing of the foot with the center of the key covered by your right-hand third finger.

When you disassemble the flute, simply follow the above instructions in reverse, always being careful not to grip the keys.

Never apply force when assembling or dissembling your flute and never rest the flute on your knee for leverage when assembling or disassembling the instrument. The entire instrument bends easily and can take on a slight banana shape.

Swab out the instrument and wipe off the lip plate before closing your case.

5 HANDS ON

Holding the flute to play feels very awkward when you're first starting out. Although it gets easier the more you play, a few simple pointers will help keep you comfortable right from the start.

Although it feels as though the flute is going to flip out of your hands at any moment, it's actually quite secure. Three stability points – on your jaw, your left hand, and your right thumb – hold it firmly in place.

Whether you are standing or sitting, remember to twist your body slightly at the waist, so that your lower half is turned slightly to the right and your upper half slightly to the left as you play. This position helps keep your shoulders and arms relaxed and allows you to breathe deeply and freely.

⑥ WELCOME TO THE FAMILY

Before we delve into playing, you should get acquainted with the various members of the flute family. Their shapes and sizes come as a big surprise to most people. So does the range of sound. When we talk about the flute, we are usually referring to the three-octave "C flute," the most common member of the flute family.

The C flute is also known as the "transverse" flute, to distinguish it from its older cousin, the recorder. This is the flute everyone starts out playing, the one you see in a concert band or an orchestra, although many pieces call for piccolo as well. Some pieces, though not that many, require one of the other members of the family.

The range of the C flute is shown below. As mentioned in Tip 3, some flutes include the extension to low B.

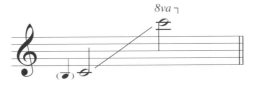

7 THE PICCOLO, ALTO, AND BASS

The piccolo is the highest and smallest member of the flute family, measuring in at 12 to 13 inches in length. It is pitched one octave above the flute, produces a piping, focused sound, and shares fingerings with the C flute. Most of the music written for band and orchestra requires just one piccolo, although a few, most notably John Philip Sousa's march "The Stars and Stripes Forever," call for multiple piccolos.

Piccolos can be made of wood, plastic, or a combination of wood or plastic with silver. The plastic is a vulcanized rubber that is often called resonite or ebonite. It's the same substance out of which bowling balls, clarinet mouthpieces, and pipe stems are made.

Wooden piccolos are very susceptible to damage from changes in temperature and moisture and should not, as a rule, be played out-of-doors. Like wooden oboes, clarinets, and bassoons, wooden piccolos should always be protected from temperature extremes and the wood should be treated with oil occasionally to help prevent cracks.

Piccolos pitched in D♭ were once used in bands. Although they're not manufactured anymore, one will occasionally turn up at garage sale, flea market, or online auction site. If you're buying a used piccolo, make sure the instrument is in the key of C before you purchase it.

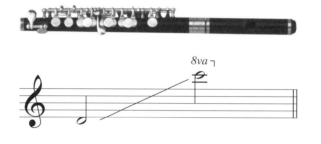

This is the written range. The piccolo sounds one octave higher than the printed notes.

The alto flute, in G, is just what the name implies – the alto of the flute family. Longer and thicker than the C flute, it sounds a fourth lower the standard flute and produces a darker, huskier sound than the C flute.

The bass flute, in the key of C, has a crooked (pronounced like "hooked"), or curved, head joint to make the length of the instrument manageable. It sounds one octave lower that the C flute and has a more diffuse sound than its higher relatives. The range of the bass flute varies depending on the instrument and the player.

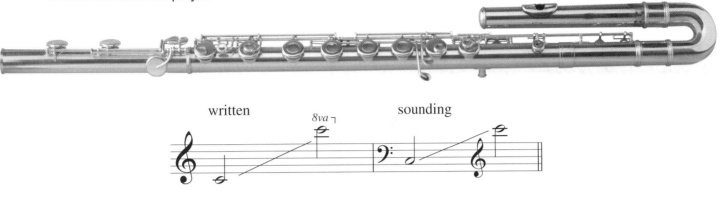

Like the piccolo, the alto and bass flutes share fingerings with the C flute.

TRACK 1	TRACK 2	TRACK 3	TRACK 4
C flute	**piccolo**	**alto flute**	**bass flute**

8 A FEW MORE FLUTES

A smaller flute in the key of E♭ was used in school band programs at one time, because its size made it easier for young students to handle. Today, children who have difficulty handling the C flute use a crooked, or curved, head joint on a C flute to shorten the instrument until they can hold it comfortably.

A B♭ flute, sometimes called a tenor flute, has a slightly stronger low-register sound than the C flute. It is usually found in the hands of jazz players because it shares a key signature with the clarinet and tenor sax, which makes it easier for players to double on the three instruments. The range of the B♭ flute is given below.

The flute family also includes a contra-alto, contrabass, double contrabass, and hyperbass flute. Although you can play a long career on the flute and never touch one of these rarely used flutes, if you ever have a chance to handle and/or play one, by all means do so. They're a lot of fun to play with and the sounds are fascinating. A YouTube search for "contrabass flute" will give you several videos of these instruments.

Flutist and composer Paige Dashner Long with (from left to right) a double contrabass flute, a sub contrabass flute, and a contrabass flute.

9 FINDING A FLUTE – RENTING

Getting a flute into your life means either buying, borrowing, or renting one. If you have a used instrument at your disposal to borrow, or perhaps one that's been in the attic for a while, you will need to have a technician go over it to make sure it's in good working order before you start playing. There's nothing quite as frustrating as struggling with an instrument that's not working correctly.

Renting can be a great option as you start out. Most music stores rent instruments for reasonable rates. In many cases, the store will offer some sort of rent-to-own program as well. Renting can be an easy, commitment-free way to get your feet wet and see how you enjoy the instrument, as well as the process of studying and practicing.

10 BUYING A FLUTE

Buying a flute can be as simple as going to the local music store and making a purchase, or it can involve checking out many stores, many brands, and many instruments. It helps to have someone you trust to help you with the purchase, perhaps your flute teacher or a flutist you know. This person can be your "second set of ears," listening to you play the instrument before you buy it. They can also advise you on good brands to look for and good outlets for finding instruments.

Beware of off-brand and imported flutes. Getting an inexpensive flute that was made on the other side of the planet is probably not a great idea. It can be impossible to get replacement parts for these instruments, in which case your cheap flute becomes worthless the moment it needs a part.

Don't be afraid to consider a used instrument. You can often get a better flute than you would otherwise think of looking at if you go with a used instrument. Again, get the advice of your teacher or another flutist. Have them ask around to see who might be selling an instrument. Always have a technician look at a used instrument before you buy it so that you know if needs any immediate work and if it's worth the asking price.

11 STUDENT, STEP-UP, OR PROFESSIONAL?

You will be looking for a "C flute," which means a flute in the key of C. Band flutes, orchestra flutes, and the vast majority of flutes you will ever come across in your life are C flutes. You may see a few wooden flutes as you start looking for an instrument. Although wooden flutes were once quite common, flutists today play metal instruments – usually silver ones – unless they are playing in an early music ensemble that specializes in music written before about 1650, or in some folk, Celtic, or other world music groups. Your musical interests may lead you to a wooden flute at some point, but a standard, metal C flute is your best and least expensive bet as you begin.

The most basic flutes on the market are **student flutes**. These are sturdy instruments that are plated in silver and stand up to uncertain handling by student hands. Make sure there is a repair person in your area who can work on the brand of flute you choose and is certain he or she can get parts for the instrument.

Step-up flutes are designed for advanced students. They are lighter and more delicate and produce a better, more flexible sound that student flutes. Many of these instruments have solid silver head joints and some have solid silver bodies as well. Someone who goes on to major in music education or plays as a hobby might never need to move beyond a good step-up flute.

Some step-up flutes are called pre-professional, and sport a few more features or characteristics of a professional flute. They are more finely crafted than the lower-level step-up instruments and produce more colorful, more flexible sound. They are also more delicate and must be handled carefully.

Professional flutes are handmade of precious metals, such as silver, gold, and platinum (solid metals – no plating), and are much more delicate than the student and step-up flutes. They make a much more flexible, colorful sound than lesser flutes and carry a much heftier price tag.

12 SOLID SILVER OR PLATED?

Deciding on a solid silver or silver plated instrument isn't an issue for someone in the market for a student flute. For the sake of durability, student flutes are nearly always made with a body constructed of a metal that is harder than silver, with silver plating applied over that body.

For beginning flutists with extremely acidic skin, or those who have experienced skin reactions from contact with certain metals, it may be advisable to put a solid silver head joint on a student flute.

Step-up flutes are available with a solid silver head joint on a silver plated body, or solid silver head joint, body, and foot joint. When considering a step-up flute, remember that solid silver flutes are much softer than the student flute you're used to handling and much more prone to denting and bending.

Most professional flutes are solid silver. Some professional flutes are made of solid gold or platinum. Flutes of these different metals make subtly different sounds than silver flutes. The price difference between silver instruments and those made of gold or platinum is not the least bit subtle.

13 OPEN OR CLOSED HOLES?

Plateau keys, or closed holes, are found on all student flutes, some step-up flutes, and a few professional instruments. The term refers to the keys operated by the second and third fingers of a flutist's left hand and the keys operated by the first, second, and third fingers of the player's right hand and means that there is no hole in the key that flutist must cover.

Open-hole flutes feature holes in the keys mentioned above. Some flutists will tell you open holes make the flute more resonant, others will tell you that open holes make playing in tune difficult. Some flutists will tell you that open holes present ergonomic issues that can lead to repetitive-use injuries (such as tendonitis or ulnar nerve entrapment) over time. Open holes are necessary to achieve some of the fingerings and effects required in the performance of new/avant garde music. In the U.S., the vast majority of professional players use open hole flutes and most students move to open holes with their step-up flutes.

Make the open hole/closed hole decision with the help and input of your teacher. Remember that once you purchase an open-hole flute, there will be a period of adjustment during which you will keep "plugs" in the open holes, removing them one at a time and adjusting that open key before moving on to the next one.

open-hole flute

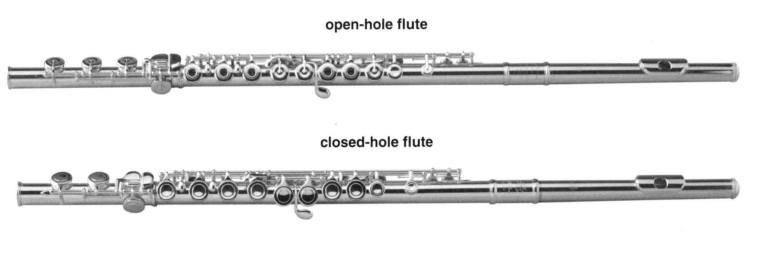

closed-hole flute

14 THE INLINE/OFFSET G DEBATE

The issue of a "dropped G key" or "offset G key" is sort of a recent development in the flute world. For many years, students played on dropped/offset G flutes, on which the G key is pushed away from the line of keys on the instrument to make it more reachable for young players. Flutists moved to an inline G when they moved to step-up and professional flutes. Students didn't move to a step-up flute until their hands could comfortably handle the inline G.

Today, open hole step-up and professional flutes are available with either an inline or dropped/offset G key. There is no difference in sound between the two models, but the dropped key can be much more comfortable for players with smaller hands. Much attention has been given to playing-related injuries in recent years, including those most likely to affect flutists: carpal tunnel syndrome, tendonitis, and ulnar nerve problems. The offset G may help reduce strain and therefore prevent such repetitive motion injuries in some players.

15 THAT PESKY E

High E is a notoriously touchy note on the flute. In order to make it more stable, some flutes are equipped with either a split E or an E ring. Both the split E and the E ring provide a way to produce high E more easily. Both present some issues, including the pitch of that E. Speak to your teacher, try several flutes with and without these options, and talk to other players before making a decision. If you're looking at a used flute that has neither option, don't worry: flute players have been learning to control high Es on modern flutes for more than a century. You will, too.

16 BEST FOOT FORWARD

Student flutes are equipped with a foot joint to allow the flute a lowest note of middle C, while step-up and professional flutes have a longer foot joint that reaches to the B one half-step below middle C.

In addition to providing the flute with a low B, the B foot adds a hidden benefit. The additional length added to the instrument warms and strengthens the instrument's sound a bit, most noticeably in the high and low extremes of the flute's range.

The reasons for not including the low B on a student flute include the weight it adds to an instrument that can already be awkward for young players to hold and balance. The bigger reason is that young players have no need to play a low B. Therefore, the added expense of including the low B would be pointless.

B foot joint

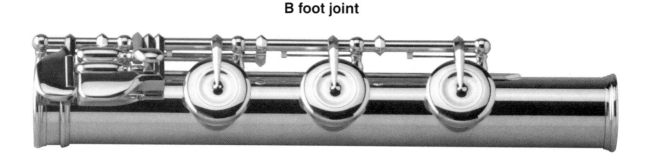

C foot joint

17 WARM UP BODY AND HANDS

Athletes warm up before they play their sport. Dancers warm up before they take class, rehearse, or perform. Actors and public speakers warm up their voices before stepping onstage in front of an audience. It should come as no surprise that musicians warm up before playing.

Start by warming up your body, with a few gentle stretches of the arms, shoulders, and neck – the same sort of stretches you might do before going out for a run. Gentle movements are the key. You are simply loosening up and getting the blood flowing. You may repeat these stretches during practice sessions if you start feeling muscle tension.

Finger stretches are a little more unique than those covering the big muscles. If your hands are cold, the best way to warm them up is to get blood flowing to them. After doing your big-muscle stretches, drop your hands to your sides with arms limp and relaxed. Make sure your hands are limp and relaxed, too. Gently flop your arms and hands about as though they have no muscles in them at all. You can feel the blood flowing into your hands and warming them almost immediately. This too can be repeated at any time if your hands start feeling cold. Wearing a sweater, or simply long sleeves, will help keep your arms and hands warm.

The best, most relaxing finger stretch involves touching your fingertips together as though there is a grapefruit between your hands. Slowly and gently, press the fingers of both hands together, while pulling your palms apart. When the fingers of both hands are touching, roll your hands slowly and gently from side to side to stretch the muscles in all of the fingers. This can be repeated at any time, if you feel your hands become tense.

Your lips should also get a little relaxing stretch. Shape your lips as though you are saying a sustained "oo" sound. Your teeth should be parted just a bit. Now, slowly and gently, drop your jaw as you move your lips to a wide "ah" shape. Feel the gentle stretch of facial and lip muscles and feel the blood flowing into those muscles. This stretch, which can be repeated at any time as you play, looks a lot like a head-splitting yawn. Remember to cover your mouth or duck behind your music stand before doing this stretch onstage or in a rehearsal, to avoid looking bored with what's going on around you.

18 WARMING UP YOUR FLUTE

Just as you need to be warmed up to play well, your flute needs to be warm as well. A cold flute tends to be flat in pitch and is less responsive than a warm flute. When a flute is extremely cold, the oil on the keys can thicken a bit, causing diminished response in the keys.

The best solution is to keep your flute from getting cold in the first place, which makes a good case for never leaving it in a vehicle or traveling with it in your trunk in cold weather. That said, taking your flute to a lesson, rehearsal, or gig on a cold winter day is likely going to mean that you will arrive with a cold flute. When this happens, open the case and give the flute a few minutes to warm up to something close to room temperature. Put the instrument together, hold it as though you're going to play and depress all the keys except the G♯ and D♯ keys. Cover the lip plate with your mouth and blow a slow, steady stream of the warmest air you can produce – as though you're steaming up a mirror. Do this several times. If the place where you are waiting before going onstage to play is cold, repeat the process just before you play.

19 HABIT FORMING

Playing a musical instrument depends on developing good habits. These habits range from handling the flute correctly and cleaning it out before packing it away to the way we sit when we play, the way we practice, the way we hold the flute and breathe, and how we use our embouchure.

Paying attention to details and learning good habits saves you the frustration and wasted time of having to unlearn and relearn something rather than just getting in the habit of doing it correctly from the beginning.

Developing a habit of regular, efficient practice is the only way to master your instrument, or for that matter, to tackle any skill you decide to master. Once you are in the habit of practicing on a regular (hopefully daily) basis, the few days on which you don't practice will feel oddly empty and incomplete.

20 CHROMATIC SCALE

As scales go, the chromatic scale is the easiest for flutists to learn. Although a single-octave chromatic scale contains more notes than a major or minor scale – 13 instead of 8 – once you learn one chromatic scale, you know them all. Play the B♭ chromatic scale that follows, as it's written. Then play the G chromatic as written. No matter which note of the chromatic scale you choose to start with, the notes always follow, ascending or descending, in half-step increments. Once you have one chromatic scale under your fingers, all you need to remember to play all the other chromatic scales (you can begin on any note) is which note you started on. It will also be your ending note.

TRACK 5

B♭ chromatic scale

This is a good spot to explain enharmonic notes. Every note in the chromatic scale goes by a few different names. B♭ can also be A♯. C♯ can also be D♭.

G chromatic scale – enharmonic spelling

21 FIRST FEW NOTES WARM-UP

The first notes you play each day are sort of a reintroduction to the flute. You are reminding your lips, lungs, arms, and hands what they need to do in order to play well. Most players do the same routine every day, from the first notes they play all the way through their warm-up. Consistency of warm-ups leads to consistency in technique and sound.

For your first notes of the day, take that G chromatic scale in Tip 20 and play it, ascending and descending, just one octave, in slurred quarter notes at a moderate tempo and at a medium volume (mezzo forte). Then play it again, loudly (forte), slurring the notes and breathing where you need to.

"Happy Birthday" is in a major key. "When Johnny Comes Marching Home Again" is in a minor key. Those two songs help to explain the character of major and minor keys. Major keys have a bright or happy character, while minor keys have a darker, more solemn character.

You should practice several of your major scales every day, remembering that the vast majority of the music you play will be constructed of major or minor scales and arpeggios. As you advance, you will begin to work on your minor scales as well. The more fluent you are in your scales and key signatures, the more quickly you will master new pieces.

B major (same fingering as C♭ major)

F♯ major (same fingering as G♭ major)

C♯ major (same fingering as D♭ major)

23 MAJOR SCALE WARM-UPS

Your scales are not only the basis for most of the music you will play, but they can serve as warm-ups and exercises that allow you to work on several facets of your playing at once. Using major scales as a sound warm up, which involves playing two octaves of the scale, ascending and descending, in long tones, is a great way to warm up your lungs, embouchure, and hands for playing. It's also a calming, mind-clearing warm-up that gets your mind focused on the work you're about to do. But wait – there's more! Using the scales in this fashion also helps make their fingering patterns second nature, which makes it easier to learn and perform music that's based on the scales. Win, win, win!

Pick two scales each day and play two octaves, ascending and descending, with the pattern below. Start at ♩ = 92 and work to slow that tempo every week or so. This builds endurance and breath control.

TRACK 6

Moderately (♩ = 92)

repeat 8va

24 CHROMATIC SCALE SOUND WARM-UP

Although all three registers of the flute have a different sound quality, from dark and warm in the low register to brilliant and ringing up high, we want to have the same control over our sound in each register. One great way to work on this is to play an octave of your chromatic scale in long tones, working to make each note as pure and strong as the note before and after it. Don't worry about tempo in this warm-up, just hold each note until you're happy with the sound and then move on. Start this warm-up on a different note each day. Be sure to reach well into the high and low registers with this warm-up each week.

25 FAST FINGERS WARM-UP

Flutes play fast notes, tubas play slow notes. Okay, that's a gross generalization, but there is some truth in it. As a flutist, you will be called upon to play fast, running passages on a regular basis. To play running notes evenly and smoothly, you need to work on that kind of playing every day. In addition to playing your scales quickly, doing several two-octave ascending and descending repetitions, you can zoom in on problems areas with the following exercise. It uses the first five notes of each major scale, repeated in 16th notes.

As you're learning this exercise, set your metronome at ♩ = 80. As it becomes comfortable, speed it up a bit each week. As it becomes comfortable, speed it up a bit each week. You will hear a lot of flutists use this warm-up, or some variation of it. It's the first five notes of each major scale, ascending by half steps. You will memorize this warm-up by repetition. Until that happens, refer to pages 23 and 24 for your scales.

TRACK 7

Fast fingers (♩ = 80)

26 TONGUING

In order produce a clean, controlled sound on the flute, you must learn to articulate – or tongue – notes. It's really as easy as saying "too" on the beginning of each note – minus the vocal sound. Your tongue should touch the roof of your mouth, slightly behind your front teeth, just as though you're saying the letter T. Say "too" several times and then pick up your flute and try tonguing a middle-register G a few times.

To warm up and hone your tonguing, take one of the major scales and play it ascending or descending, using the tonguing pattern below: Choose a different scale each day, making your way through all the scales before starting over again. Be sure to alternate registers so that you cover the entire range of the flute over the course of a week.

TRACK 8

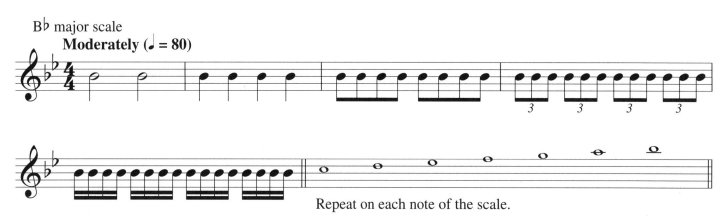

Repeat on each note of the scale.

27 EMBOUCHURE

The word embouchure is a bit of a catchall, referring to what all wind and brass players do with their mouths to create sound. For flutists, the general rule is that you want to place the embouchure hole of the instrument on the center of your bottom lip with the bottom edge of the hole on the line of your lower lip. However, differences in dental configuration and the fact that not everyone can create a perfectly centered aperture with their lips means that some people will place the embouchure hole slightly to one side of center. If you are someone with an offset embouchure and are worried about it holding you back, take note that Marcel Moyse, one of the most famous flutists and teachers of the 20th century, played with an offset embouchure.

Some teachers will ask you to use a flexible, mobile embouchure, shaping sound differently in each of the three octaves of the flute. Others may ask you to keep your lips relatively still as you play. Remember that what matters is not what an embouchure looks like, but the sound it produces. Your embouchure is working well if you can make a clean, in-tune sound in all three octaves of the flute's range.

To warm up your embouchure, play the following exercise, practicing moving smoothly and evenly from note to note. When the exercise becomes easy to play well at the marked tempo, speed it up a bit and continue working. When that becomes easy, speed it up again, etc.

TRACK 9

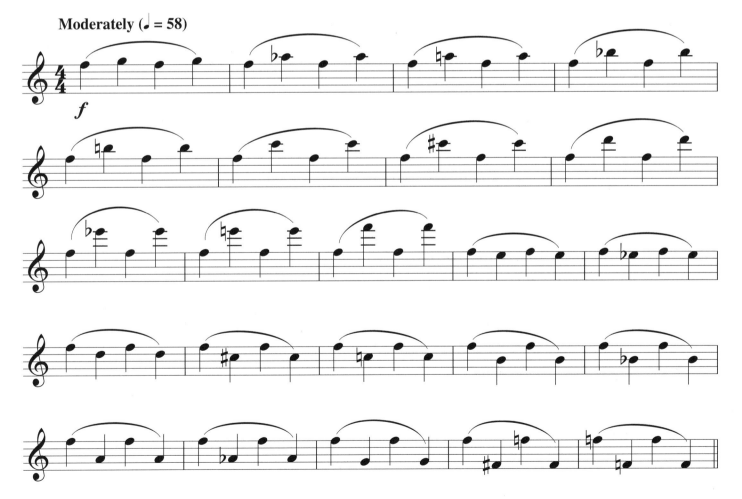

DYNAMITE DYNAMICS

One of the elements that makes a musician's playing interesting is his or her use of dynamics, or gradations of volume. Artful use of dynamics includes extremes of soft and loud playing as well as movement from one dynamic level or another.

You will often see markings in your music directing you to play loudly or softly.

term	written	played
fortissimo	***ff***	very loud
forte	***f***	loud
mezzo forte	***mf***	moderately loud
mezzo piano	***mp***	moderately soft
piano	***p***	soft
pianissimo	***pp***	very soft
fortepiano	***fp***	loud then soft

You will also see marks indicating that you should *crescendo* (increase) or *diminuendo* (decrease) the volume of sound you are making over the course of several beats.

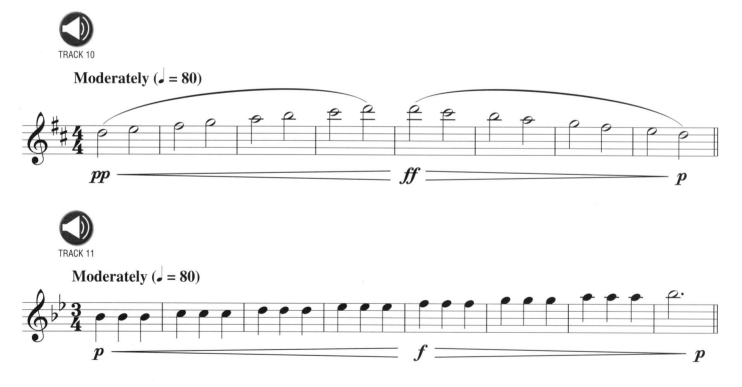

You may also see instructions that tell you make a sudden, big change in dynamic level, such as the *sforzando* in Track 12 or the *subito piano* in Track 13.

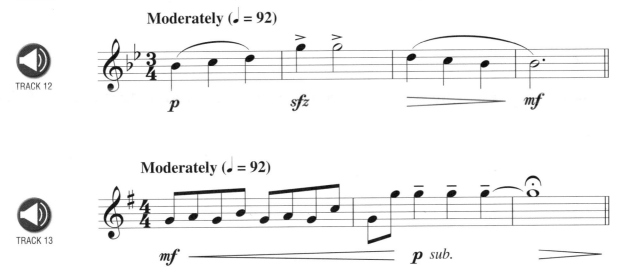

Practicing dynamics shifts as part of your daily routine is the best way to ensure that you are ready with these important musical tools when you need to use them. As you play your major scales, for finger technique and tonguing, use them as dynamic exercises as well. You may *crescendo* and *diminuendo* over the course of the scales, or play as loudly or softly as possible for an entire scale.

TIPS 29 – 32 TEACHERS AND LESSONS

29 HELP ME, PLEASE

Any musician will tell you that musical progress comes through diligent, disciplined practice. A good teacher is someone who can listen to what you're doing and help you identify what and how to practice to improve your playing. Find the best teacher you can, one who has solid credentials and experience and one you are comfortable working with.

Remember that you are the consumer when you take a lesson. You are not just there to play well for your teacher, you are there to learn and take that knowledge out the door with you. Keep a notebook and take notes on each lesson. Some teachers will want you to do this in the lesson, others may prefer that you wait until the lesson is over.

30 WHO SAID THAT?

When you work on a piece of music with a teacher and he or she makes musical suggestions and/or makes marks in your music, add the teacher's initials to those markings. Years down the road, you may find yourself passing that teacher's ideas to one of your own students.

31 WHO'S WHO

There is a difference between a coach and a teacher. A flute teacher can delve into issues specific to the flute and work with you over a long period of time to develop your playing. A coach does not need to be a flutist to give you musical insights on specific music you're preparing. In fact, a coach who is a pianist or string player will listen to your playing without any regard to the technical concerns of the instrument, which is also how your audience will hear you. This can be terrifically valuable.

32 AN ISSUE OF TRUST

You have to trust your teacher, but you also have to be a critical thinker. It's perfectly fine to disagree with your teacher on an interpretive decision. However, if you find yourself disagreeing constantly with your teacher, or if you feel you are no longer learning from your teacher, perhaps it's time to find someone new. Remember that you are the consumer in the relationship with your teacher. Be respectful, but don't be afraid to switch teachers if need be.

TIPS 33 – 38 : LEARNING

33 BE YOUR OWN TEACHER

Although you can't replace the insights you can get from someone who has years of training and experience on your instrument, you can learn a lot about your own playing just by listening to yourself. The key to this kind of listening is to record yourself and then to give your undivided attention to the recording.

Listening to the recording right after you play something can be helpful, showing you little flaws that you might have missed while you were concentrating on playing. But if you wait a day or two before listening, you may be very surprised by what you hear. Often, the musical statements we think we are making are not as strong as we hoped when we hear them on a recording. Putting a little time between playing and listening helps you to hear those sorts of details clearly.

Playing for people whose opinions you trust is also a good way of learning what your audience is hearing in your playing. In addition, playing for a critique in this way is also a good means for getting performance nerves out of the way.

34 FINGERING CHARTS

Fingering charts are just what the name implies: charts that show the fingerings for each note in the flute's range. As you're learning the flute, you need to have a chart that you can refer to each time you learn a new note, as well as to refresh your memory on notes you don't use very often in your daily practice.

You can purchase a fingering chart at a music store, find one in a method book, or find one online. You can also get a smart phone app that contains one. Just make sure the one you choose makes sense to you and is easy to read.

Most fingering charts display fingerings in horizontal or vertical formats that look something like this:

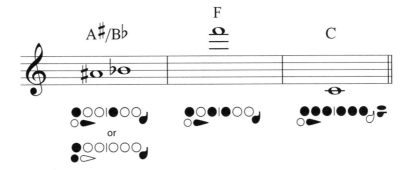

A few of the charts out there refer you back to a drawing of the flute with numbers assigned to each key. These tend to be a little hard to read and more cumbersome to use.

Write the new fingering in your music for reference as you're learning the note. Don't worry about the fingerings you don't know yet. You will learn fingerings, one at a time, in the studies and pieces you play, which is the best way to learn them. Although each new fingering will feel awkward at first, and will take a few practice sessions to remember, they will settle in quickly.

35 MAKING GOOD MARKS

It is always better to make helpful marks in your music than to make mistakes in performance. Those marks can be everything from accidentals and dynamics to little reminders of tempo changes and pitch pitfalls. Some musicians write full words in their parts, while some use little drawings, such as eyeglasses to indicate a spot where they must pay special attention to the conductor.

Always keep a pencil on your stand as you practice or rehearse. Write whatever helps you play well, but **never write in anything other than pencil.** You will not always play from music you own and you will not always need the same marks each time you return to a particular piece of music. Getting in the habit of marking in plain, No. 2 lead pencil right from the start will save you headaches later on.

 36 WRITING A WRONG

Although marking music in pencil is the way to go, storing that pencil in your case, where it can damage your flute, is a really bad idea. Keep your pencil in your zippered case cover or in whatever bag you use to carry music.

 37 LISTEN!

In many ways, you are going to be your own best teacher. By listening to as much music as you can, both live and recorded, you will internalize rhythms, styles, musical phrases, and many more expressive and technical details of making music.

Listening to recordings is a great way to hear some of the world's great flutists. Some of the names to look for in classical recordings include Jean-Pierre Rampal, James Galway, Paula Robison, Jeanne Baxtresser, and Emmanuel Pahud.

Some big jazz names are Herbie Mann, Hubert Laws, Nestor Torres, and Jerome Richardson.

In the rock world – yes there is some flute in the rock world – look for recordings of the band Jethro Tull and its flutist, Ian Anderson, as well as recordings by jazz/rock fusion flutist Tim Weisberg.

These are just suggestions for starters. Listen to as many flutists as you can.

 38 READ!

Understanding music goes much deeper than playing notes on your flute. You can spend a lifetime exploring, enjoying, and learning about music. In addition to practicing, taking lessons, and listening to performances and recordings, you should be reading.

Many musicians absolutely swear by Barry Green and W. Timothy Gallwey's book *The Inner Game of Music*, as a guide to developing focus and discipline and overcoming performance anxiety. Some musicians prefer W. Timothy Gallwey, Zach Kleiman, and Pete Carroll's original book, *The Inner Game of Tennis*, adapting its principles to their musical endeavors. Either way, the books are worth perusing.

Malcolm Galdwell's *Outliers: The Story of Success* explores the question: "What makes successful people successful?" His 10,000-hour rule, which effectively states that you cannot master a thing until you have spent 10,000 hours working at it, is an inspiration to practice.

From Robert Greenberg's *How to Listen to Great Music* to Daniel J. Levitin's *This Is Your Brain on Music*, to books on every genre of music and on hundreds of composers, songwriters, lyricists, and performers, countless books have been written on the subject of music. Find books that speak to your musical interests and start reading. The more you know about music, the more you bring to the music you play.

39 BEYOND THE NOTES TO MAKING MUSIC

Technical perfection is a great thing. By all means, clean up the rhythms and notes of the pieces you're working on. Once you've done that, it's time to make them your own – to make musical statements with them. Making a piece your own means giving each phrase meaning with dynamic changes, accents, and a sense of the direction of each phrase.

Listen to the following two examples of "Amazing Grace." The first one is played without thought to making music: the second is played with musical expression.

🔊 **Without expression**

TRACK 14

🔊 **With expression**

TRACK 15

A good way to practice making music instead of just playing notes is to take a melody, perhaps a favorite song or an old folk tune, and try playing it many different ways. As you play "Amazing Grace" yourself, experiment with making a *crescendo*, or growing louder, over the course of one line of the song. And then try it with a *diminuendo*. You can add or subtract accents as you experiment and you can play with your use of vibrato. Listen to recordings of the song and decide which ones you like best. Ask yourself why you like some recordings more than others, and see if you can bring some elements of those performances into your own performance. Don't be afraid to hum or sing the music a few times.

AMAZING GRACE

Words by John Newton
Traditional American Melody

40 MEMORIZE, TRANSPOSE, AND PLAY BY EAR

Although learning to read music is absolutely essential, learning to memorize, improvise, and play by ear are important skills, too. They give you command over the pieces you play and they free you from always being glued to a sheet of music as you play. Start your memorization with the simple, familiar melody "Amazing Grace," which you worked on in the previous tip, and memorize it phrase by phrase. When you have memorized the first phrase, add the second, and so on.

Once you've memorized the melody, play it several times from memory. Now try playing it in a different key. You are relying on your ear to guide you, which is great training for your ear.

Now try playing the melody in Track 16 by ear. It's okay to play the track several times, and to sing or hum it before you try to repeat it.

Flow Gently, Sweet Afton
Music by Alexander Hume

TRACK 16

41 SILENCE IS GOLDEN

You are playing a wind instrument, so you need to breathe. But you do not need to make unnecessary noise while breathing. Some teachers will tell you to open your throat and think of yawning as you breathe, others will tell you to imagine your mouth, throat, and lungs as a giant tunnel through which the air will flow. Whatever image you choose to conjure, you must get in the habit of taking, large, fast, relaxed breaths that create as little sound as possible.

If you concentrate on deep, silent breathing during your warm-ups and practice sessions, you will carry the habit into your playing as well.

 THERE'S NO PAUSE BUTTON

Everyone who teaches a wind instrument has seen a student take a deep breath and then freeze, waiting for several beats to pass before it's time to play. While the deep breath part of this scenario is a good thing, the tension created by holding that breath is a bad thing. You want to breathe in tempo, on the last beat or two before you have play, making an immediate turnaround with that air. You should begin playing the moment you're done inhaling.

 LONG TONES

Getting a lot of air into your body, smoothly, is exactly half of the battle. You must also exhale in a smooth, controlled fashion. Long tones are the best exercise for hearing whether your breath support is strong and even. Play the following exercise every day, starting on different notes in different octaves each time. Do some of the groupings with vibrato and some without, always listening for a smooth, even sound. Start at ♩ = 104 and slow it down a bit every few weeks to increase lung capacity and stability of sound.

TRACK 17

Moderately (♩ = 104)

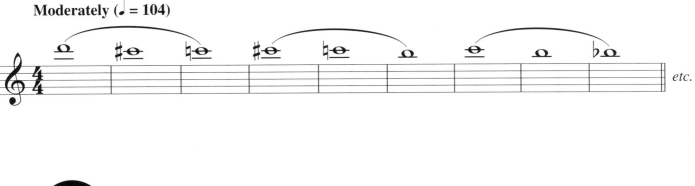

etc.

PRACTICE BREATING?

It's true that you've known how to breathe from the moment you were born. It's also true that you now need to get control over something you have been doing without thinking, every hour of every day of your life. Whether you are playing long tones, scales, pieces you're learning, or things you're sight-reading, you must always breathe in tempo, in appropriate, unobtrusive spots in the music and without making distracting sounds.

Mark the spots in which you plan to breathe by placing a mark slightly above the line of music in the exact spot at which you plan to take a breath. Most wind players and singers use one of the following marks: ' or √ or ∨. Once the breath is marked, always breathe in that spot, whether you are playing the entire piece, or just repeating small sections of it as you practice. That way, the breaths become a part of the way you play the piece.

 IN GOES THE GOOD AIR...

You can work on increasing the amount of air you take in with each breath with this simple exercise: Relax and exhale whatever air is in your lungs. Take three consecutive breaths, without exhaling in between. Think about filling up your lungs by a third with each breath. After the final inhale, your lungs should feel very full. Still without exhaling, take two short sniffs through your nose before exhaling on a slow hiss. As you take the sniffs of air, you should feel slightly over full of air. Do not do this exercise more than two times in a row, to avoid becoming lightheaded.

TIPS 46 – 53 : PRACTICING

 KEEP A "LATER" LIST

Keep a bit of paper handy for stray thoughts as you sit down to practice. You need to focus on your warm-up and practice session in order to get any work done, which means you can't be thinking about the fact that you need to put gas in the car or what should be on the grocery list or who you need to call. As those thoughts bubble up – and they will – write them down. When you're done practicing, you can pick up the list and deal with whatever had crossed your mind earlier. Writing those thoughts down allows you to let go of them while you're practicing and clear your mind for the work at hand.

 KEEP A "TO DO" LIST

In the same way that committing stray thoughts to paper will help you focus as you practice, having a clear set of goals will help keep your practice session on track. Keep notes on what music needs to be ready next, what music you have to prepare in the coming weeks, which warm-ups you want to do each day, and which ones you want to alternate.

Leave a little time on the list for fun – playing a piece you know well and really enjoy, playing something new that interests you, and taking a moment to play a tune or two by ear or improvise on a tune you know well.

PRACTICE CAN MAKE IMPERFECT

If you keep making the same mistake every time you play a passage in a piece of music, you are effectively practicing that mistake and making it a permanent fixture in that piece. When you make a mistake, stop and mark it. Even if you don't have time to work on it at that moment, you have flagged the spot as a problem. When you sit down to practice, always check your music for the problems you have marked. Pull them out of context and fix them. This may sound like a complex task, but it's actually quite straightforward.

Let's say this passage – from one of G.F. Handel's flute sonatas – is giving you trouble:

Play it several times and pay attention to exactly where the problem occurs. You will begin to notice that most problem passages are really just problems getting from one single note to the next one. Aha! Isolate the two notes and go back and forth between them at a slow tempo until you can play them comfortably. Gradually add notes on either side of the problem. Remember that if you can't play something correctly at a slow tempo, you're not going to be able to play it correctly at a fast tempo either. Gradually (notch by notch on your metronome) speed it up. As you are working on speeding up the passage, try altering the rhythm to keep your mind alert and to help get the passage under your fingers. The following two exercises focus on measures 3 and 4.

TRACK 19

TRACK 20

Take note: digital metronomes move up in single beats-per-minute increments. Most musicians stick to the original metronome marking system, which makes moves in several-beat increments, as follows: 40, 42, 44, 46, 48, 50, 52, 54, 56, 58, 60, 63, 66, 69, 72, 76, 80, 84, 88, 92, 96, 100, 104, 108, 112, 116, 120, 126, 132, 138, 144, 152, 160, 168, 176, 184, 192, 200, 208.

If your metronome does not move in these increments, simply increase by four or five beats per minute as you speed things up.

(49) BUSY, BUSY, BUSY

We're all busy. Your practice time is precious and needs to be used well. Efficient practicing means you are not repeating mistakes. You want to locate the mistakes and work them out. Playing a passage correctly after working on it is great, but it's not the end of the road. Some teachers will tell you that you have fixed a problem when you can play the problem spot five times in a row with no mistakes. Other teachers will say ten times in a row. Either way, the point remains the same – you have to be able to play a section correctly multiple times in a row, and to do that for several days in a row, before it is really secure.

50 BREAKING UP IS NOT HARD TO DO

When you are working on a piece of music, remember that you are really working on several different issues: rhythm, notes (fingerings), sound, and musical expression. There is no law that says you have to work on all four issues at once. In fact, you will work more efficiently if you break the music into individual components. It's best to work on the individual elements of piece in the order listed above (rhythm, notes, sound, musical expression). The rhythm provides an essential structure. Work out the rhythm without the flute in your hands. Once you can tap, clap, or speak the rhythm accurately, pick up the flute and start working on getting the passage under your fingers. After you have the rhythm and notes under control, you can start working on playing the passage with a colorful, clear sound, which leads nicely to working on dynamics and other expressive details.

51 WORKING ON RHYTHMS

If you can't tap the rhythms you're working on, you certainly can't play them. When you are working on a new or difficult rhythm, put the flute down and set your metronome to a fairly slow tempo. Practice tapping the rhythm to the beat. Feel free to mark beat numbers in your music (in pencil, of course) or to use simple hash marks to indicate beats in the measures in question. The hash marks help you see the beats more clearly as you play.

52 MORE METRONOME IDEAS

Be creative with your use of the metronome. If you are working on a long, fast passage, subdivide it with the metronome beating every eighth note instead of every quarter. You can also set the metronome for every other beat. For example, if the tempo is ♩ = 120, set it to 60 to avoid putting stresses on each beat. Many metronomes have a setting that makes no sound but flashes a light on each beat. Use this to see where you might be rushing or dragging when not listening to the beats ticking away. It's always a good idea to work your scales, arpeggios, and tonguing exercises with a metronome, to make sure you are playing all of them evenly.

53 TO STAND OR TO SIT

Students often ask if they should stand or sit when they practice. The answer is: yes. When we play in orchestras, chamber groups, and other ensembles, we sit. When we play recitals, competitions, and auditions, we stand. You need to be secure and comfortable standing and sitting as you play, so incorporate both positions into your practice sessions. You might want to stand as you play your warm-ups, and then sit as you settle in to work on music. You may want to alternate sitting and standing as you practice to keep your energy level up. Whatever works best for you is fine, as long you do both.

TIPS 54 – 64: TAKING GOOD CARE OF YOUR FLUTE

54 CLEAN AS A WHISTLE

Never ever submerge any section of your flute in water. Never. Ever. The best way to clean your flute after playing is to swab it out with a standard flute cleaning/tuning rod and a soft cotton cloth that is neatly hemmed on all sides Many flutists use a men's cloth handkerchief as a cleaning rag – the white dress handkerchief, not the larger, brightly colored bandana-style handkerchief. Run it through the washer and dryer before using it to make sure the sizing is out of the fabric. Now you have a soft, absorbent cleaning cloth.

To clean your flute, thread a corner of your cleaning cloth through the eye on the end of the cleaning rod. Cover the top of the rod with the cloth, wrap the cloth around the rod and hold it taut against the base of the rod. As long as you continue to hold the twisted cloth in place as you swab the inside of the instrument, you are in no danger of getting the cloth wadded up and stuck inside the instrument. If it does get stuck, try to push the rod through the instrument. Trying to pull it out tends to make matters worse. If the rod and cloth ever do get hopelessly stuck in the instrument, take it to a repairperson.

Do not put your flute away while it is still wet with condensation from playing. If you do, your case will develop a bad, musty smell. Eventually that odor will cling to your flute, which, since your flute rests about an inch below your nose as you play, will be very noticeable.

Do not put your cleaning rag inside your case. It too will give your case and flute a bad, musty smell. In addition, your case is designed to fit the flute snugly and to keep it from shifting and moving. The added bulk of the cleaning cloth inside the case can bend the keys of your flute and depress the keys with enough force to damage the pads, which of course affects your sound.

You can tie the rag to the handle of your case or fold it loosely inside your zippered case cover, if you have one. If you leave it inside your case cover, be sure to leave the zipper slightly undone to allow air inside. When practicing at home, it's not a bad idea to drape the cleaning rag over your stand when you pack up, to air it out.

Launder your cleaning rag frequently. You may want to have several to rotate so that you always have a clean one ready to use.

Some music stores sell flute cleaning devices that look like over-sized pipe cleaners. They recommend that you simply insert the "pipe cleaner" into the flute and leave it there as you pack the flute away in your case. Most flutists avoid these cleaners because they trap moisture inside the case and lead to – you guessed it – a bad, musty smell in your case.

Please note that the cleaning rod has a second purpose. On the closed end of the rod you will find a line etched into the rod. This is a marking point for the position of the cork in the head joint. Insert the closed end of the cleaning rod into head joint, until you feel it hit the plate that covers the cork. The line etched in your cleaning rod should now be visible in the center of the embouchure hole. If it is not centered, either tighten the crown, or loosen it and then push it further into the head joint, to center the line. When the line is centered, the head joint is set up to facilitate in-tune playing. If the crown does not move easily, see a repair person. **Never** try to force the crown in either direction.

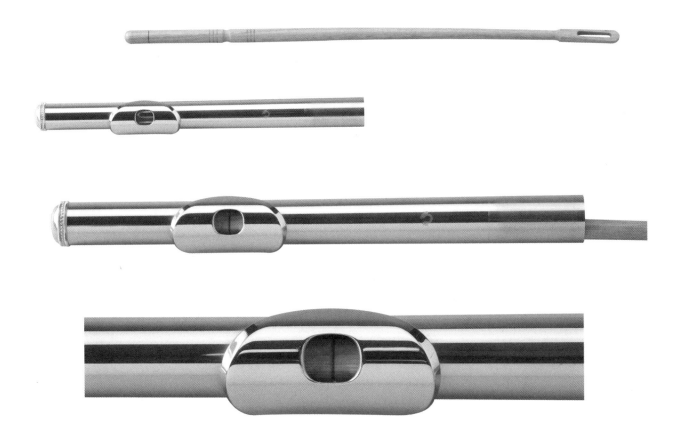

56 CAST A LITTLE LIGHT

If you find yourself with a smelly case, open it, and remove the instrument. Then lay the case on a table or other flat surface in direct sunlight for a few hours. You may have to do this for several days.

57 VITAMIN C FOR THE FLUTE

If sunlight isn't enough to freshen up your case, try placing a few pieces of fresh orange peel inside the empty case and closing it up for a few hours. The oil from the orange peel is a natural odor killer.

58 MAKE IT SHINE

Keeping your flute shiny and clean is a simple process. You can wipe it down with your moist cleaning cloth when you're done playing to remove finger prints and smudges from the metal. Periodically, you should lightly dampen a very small area of your cleaning rag with rubbing alcohol and run that area of the cloth over the body and keys of the flute. Give a little extra attention to the lip plate and embouchure hole, taking care not to scratch the edges or interior of the embouchure hole, as this can affect your sound.

Music stores sell flute polishing cloths, which are soft cloths treated with a chemical that removes tarnish from silver. Some flutists go over their flutes periodically with these cloths and some never do. Some flutists put tarnish-shield strips in the cases to stave off tarnishing. If you use these cloths or papers, keep them away from the lip plate. You don't want those chemicals on your lips and in your mouth.

Never, never use silver polish on your flute. The polish can damage the surface of the pads and clog up the ribbing, slowing down the action of the flute and making keys stick.

 59 GESUNDHEIT!

Whenever you have a cold, sore throat, or any sort of bug, the air you blow through your flute is filled with germs. If you have to play while you have a cold, keep some individually wrapped rubbing alcohol wipes in your gig bag and wipe down your lip plate and embouchure hole before your pack up your flute.

Use those wipes to rub down the lip plate and embouchure hole of anyone else's flute before you play it, as well as your own flute after someone else plays it. This will greatly reduce your chances of catching a cold and will also prevent you from picking up the HSV-1 virus, which causes cold sores.

Cold sores are miserable for anyone, but particularly so for flutists. If you have never had a cold sore, be grateful and don't share beverage containers or glasses with others, as this is the most common means of spreading the virus.

If you do get cold sores, you can prevent outbreaks by avoiding bright sunlight on your lips, or wearing a SPF 40 or greater sunblock lotion when you go out in the sun. Lips that are chapped and cracked are particularly susceptible to cold sore outbreaks, so keep lip balm handy and use it religiously.

 60 LUNCH, ANYONE?

Brush your teeth before playing, if at all possible, or at very least rinse out your mouth with water. Pay attention to what you eat in the couple of hours before you play, avoiding milk, cheese, and other dairy products as well as garlic and other pungent spices. Even if you swab the flute carefully after you play, residue from your recent meal or snack will absorb into the pads and can give a distinct odor to the flute and its case.

Wash your hands before you play. Food residue on hands will leave a film on the flute and can cause the silver to tarnish prematurely. Hand lotion can have the same effect.

 61 PADS

The pads on many flutes are made of dense felt that is covered by a delicate membrane, which resembles fine tissue paper. The pads are "seated" to make an airtight seal on the keys of your flute. They are delicate and subject to wear. If you notice a change in the tone quality of one or two notes on your flute, you probably have a pad issue or a key that has slipped out of adjustment. A good repair person can reseat a single pad, adjust a key or, if necessary, replace a damaged pad to correct the issue.

Depending on how much you play and how you handle your flute, you will probably need to have the instrument completely re-padded at some point. If you treat your flute with care and have adjustments made as needed, you should be able to make a single set of pads last for years.

A CASE FOR SAFETY

The best rule for protecting your instrument from damage is to put it safely in its case whenever you're not playing it.

Once upon a time, flutes came with stout, wooden cases that were outfitted with luggage latches. They were extremely protective, if a bit heavy. Today, the plastic cases that come with most student flutes (and many step-up flutes) are much lighter than the old wooden cases, but not nearly as protective. The biggest flaw in these cases is the latches, which are often loose. If the case opens, the flute goes flying.

You'll see a lot of flutists using zippered covers over their hard flute cases. This is more than a fashion statement. If you drop your flute case, or even bump it hard, it's entirely possible that it will pop open and scatter the instrument pieces. Aside from bending keys (the G♯ key being particularly vulnerable), hitting the ground can put bends in the tenons that connect the head joint, body, and foot joint. Although this damage can often be repaired, the flute can't be assembled until the repair is done.

The bottom line is that a zippered case cover, which surrounds the hard case and guarantees that it cannot pop open, will cost much less than the repair work the instrument will need after it hits the ground. Case covers also provide space for a cleaning rag, pencil, powdered papers, and other odds and ends between the hard case and the case cover. Several types of replacement cases are available for flutes, including foam-padded, zippered cases that also cannot pop open.

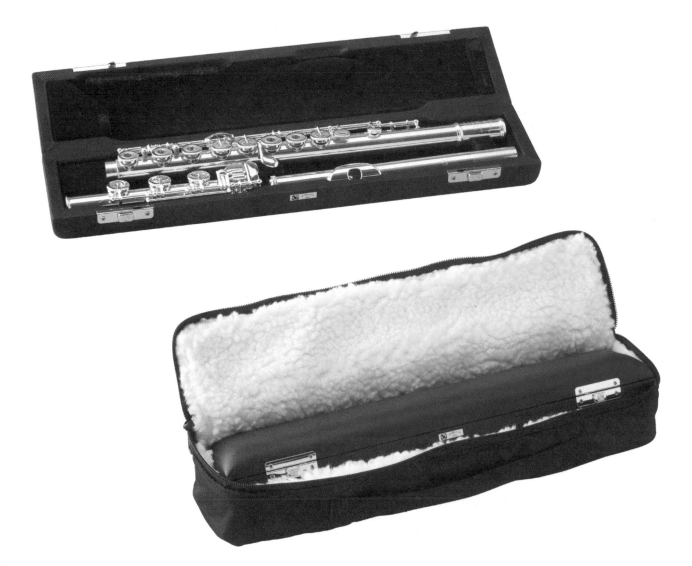

63 SAFETY FIRST!

If you leave your flute on a bed, on a chair, or on the floor, sooner or later someone will sit on it or step on it. If you leave your flute on a music stand, you run the risk of having it fall to the floor. As you might imagine, the flute will not fare well in any of these encounters.

You can safely lay a flute on a hard surface, a dresser top, a shelf or a table, as long as you set it down so that it is not resting on its keys.

incorrect

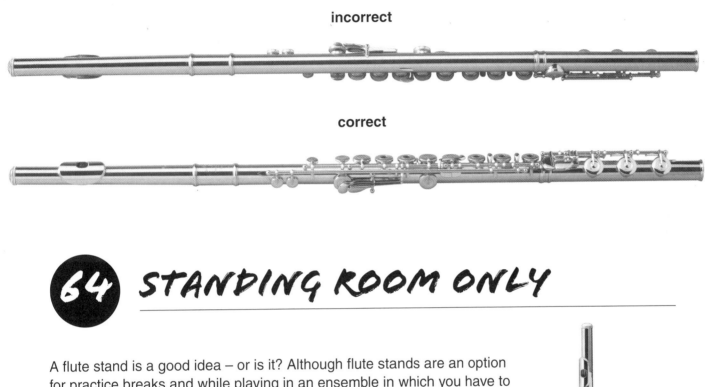

correct

64 STANDING ROOM ONLY

A flute stand is a good idea – or is it? Although flute stands are an option for practice breaks and while playing in an ensemble in which you have to play more than one instrument, a flute stand on the floor can get kicked over quite easily. It's best to keep the stand on a table or desk at home, and to never leave your flute unattended on its stand while on a job.

A piccolo on a stand can be almost invisible to someone walking by. The piccolo and its stand will go flying if kicked, so the same safety considerations that apply to flute stands apply to piccolo stands as well.

65 BE SURE OF YOUR INSURANCE

Your homeowner's or renter's insurance is probably not going to cover an instrument you use professionally. Some insurance companies will cover instruments if they are listed under a separate "rider" to a homeowner's or renter's policy. Getting an instrument listed usually requires a receipt for the purchase of the instrument or an appraisal by a qualified instrument appraiser or dealer.

If you are insuring an instrument, give some thought not only to the replacement cost of the instrument, if it is stolen or destroyed, but also to the repair cost if it is dropped, stepped on, or otherwise damaged.

Read the exclusions on your policy! Most policies will not cover instruments that are stolen from unattended vehicles, which is something you don't want to find out after your instrument has been pilfered from the trunk of your car.

66 KEEPING TABS ON YOUR FLUTE

Traveling with a musical instrument is a lot like traveling with a small child – you must always be aware of it. Any musical instrument that is packed in a case and carried around is susceptible to theft – particularly the flute, because it's so small. If you leave your case unattended on a table in a restaurant, on the counter in a restroom, or in the waiting area of a train station or airport, it can easily disappear into someone else's bag.

When carrying your flute from place to place, put the entire case in a messenger bag, backpack, or some other carrying bag that obscures the case. Keep that bag closed and with you at all times. If you're riding a train or sitting in a large public waiting area, place the bag on the floor between your feet so that you're always mindful of where it is.

Never leave your flute in a vehicle – not in the passenger compartment or in the trunk. Aside from the fact that most insurance policies won't cover it if it's heisted from a car, your flute should never be exposed to the extremes of heat and cold that can occur in an unattended vehicle.

67 CROSSING BORDERS

If you are traveling outside the country with your flute, it's a good idea to carry some proof of ownership of the instrument. A copy of a receipt for purchase or an appraisal, along with a photo of the instrument and the serial number, will do. Carry the proof of ownership separately from the instrument – it's best to keep it with your passport. If you are separated from the instrument while going through customs or if the instrument is stolen or lost while you're abroad, documentation of the instrument, including its serial number, may be the key to getting it back.

Check with your insurance agent to make sure your instrument is covered in the country/countries you plan to visit.

AIRLINES

Never assume. It's always a good idea to check with the airline you'll be using to make sure they allow musical instruments in the passenger cabin of the plane. When taking an instrument through airport security, don't be surprised if security personnel want to remove the flute from its case and take a good look at it. To avoid damage, volunteer to put it back in its case rather than letting them do it.

STICKY SITUATIONS

No matter how careful you are about food, beverages, and lip balms before you play, eventually the pads on your flute will get sticky. A sticky sound that occurs when you release a key, or a slight slowing of the key response, will be your warning that you need to dry off the surface of the pads.

Powder papers or pad cleaner/pad dryer cloths are the best solutions for drying off the pads. The paper, or cloth, is placed between the pad and the key and the key is pressed down. Always keep some sort of pad drying/cleaning papers or cloths in your gig bag. In a pinch, and only in a pinch, a very old, soft dollar bill can serve as a key drying paper. Powder papers and drying cloths can be purchased at music stores and fit easily in your case cover.

TUNING THE INSTRUMENT

Before working with another musician, or a number of other musicians, you must make sure all the instruments involved are in tune with one another. If you're working with a pianist, you may ask for an A, at which point the pianist will play the A for you and may also play the A minor chord, softly, to help you. You will also sound the A, listening to whether you are in tune with the piano, a bit above it (sharp), or a bit below it (flat). If you have difficulty telling whether you are sharp or flat, sustain the A and raise your head just slightly to raise the pitch and then lower your head just slightly to lower it. Your ears will guide you to either keep your head a little low or raise it up again to match the tuning note. If you have to raise your head to bring the flute in tune, push the head joint in just a bit, which will make the flute shorter and raise its pitch. If you had to drop your head to bring it in tune, pull the head joint out to make the flute just a bit longer and lower its pitch. Test the A against the piano again after you have moved the head joint. Adjust the head joint again if you need to. In an ensemble with a keyboard instrument, the pitch is always taken from the keyboard.

The same process works no matter which or how many instruments you are working with. In an ensemble that includes an oboe, the oboist will sound the tuning A. Each family of instruments tunes as a group. Bands use the same process, but usually tune to a B♭. If there is a piano on the stage, for a concerto, the tuning A will be taken from the piano.

# SPOT TUNING

Tuning before a concert gives everyone in the group a common starting point, but it does not guarantee good pitch throughout a concert. Only listening to each other constantly and reacting quickly can do that.

Your instrument will have individual notes that will tend to be a little sharp or a little flat. Knowing those tendencies, which you can work on with a tuner, helps you adjust before there's a problem. Knowing the tendencies of the instruments around you will also help you to adjust before there's a problem. String instruments tend to go lower, or flatter, in pitch as they warm up, while woodwinds and brass instruments tend to go higher, or sharper.

Adjusting is as simple as raising or lowering your head as you play the out-of-tune notes, just as your did when you were tuning. Remember that raising your head a little bit raises the pitch of the note you're playing, while lowering your head lowers the pitch. Do not attempt to roll the flute toward your lips or away from them. This can pinch off your sound and cause you to lose your grip on the flute.

72 WORKING WITH A TUNER

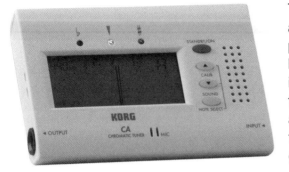

Tuners are great tools, but they cannot replace listening and adjusting to what's going on around you as you play. Playing slow scales while watching a tuner can help you identify the tendencies of your particular instrument. Many flutes tend to be a little sharp on C♯, for instance. Working your scales and arpeggios with a tuner can help you adjust your C♯s to be in tune with the rest of your scale, rather than allowing yourself to get used to the sound of a sharp C♯.

You can purchase tuners from music stores or online, but you should read the specifications and reviews and make sure the tuner functions well with the high pitches of the flute. Tuner apps are now available for smart phones, iPods, and the like. As with stand-alone tuners, read the specifications and reviews to make sure the tuner will work well with the flute. Remember, a tuner is a tool to train your ears, not a replacement for good listening skills.

73 WHAT'S THAT SOUND?

Most of us have had the experience of hearing a recording of our singing or speaking voice and feeling surprise at the quality or sound. Since what we heard on the playback is produced inside the same skull that houses our ears, it's no small wonder that our perception of our own voice is usually rather different from reality. The flute's sound may be produced outside your head, but the instrument rests on your jaw, sending sound waves along the bone to your ears. The head joint, which sits five to six inches from your ears, produces not only the flute's sound, but also a sound of rushing air. Ask a flutist friend to play something for you and then stand a few inches from the head joint of instrument as he or she plays. After listening for 30 seconds to a minute, walk a few feet away and listen. Then go a few more feet and listen again. The instrument sounds quite different as you move away from the player.

Recording yourself is a great tool for working on tone and musical expression. To make a recording that really captures what you sound like to an audience members, place the microphone at least eight feet from you. Don't listen to the recording immediately after you make it. Wait a little bit, perhaps until the end of your practice session, so that you will actually hear what you did. That little window of time can make the recording very revealing. A digital recorder or perhaps a computer program that records through a microphone should suffice. The recording quality you will get through a smart phone will probably not be good enough to really help you work on details.

Just as audio recordings can help you work on aspects of your playing, video recordings can reveal a lot of little tics that creep into one's playing over time. Foot tapping, head bobbing, noisy breathing, and sloppy posture are on the list of things that a video will reveal. You don't need great audio for this kind of recording, so don't run out and spend a lot on high-end equipment. The video capabilities of your smart phone or your point-and-shoot camera will probably do just fine for your purposes.

74 LANGUAGES IN MUSIC

How's you Italian? Your French? Your German? Singers aren't the only musicians who need a command of languages in order to perform well. Although no one is going to ask you about song lyrics in German when you show up to play your flute, you may find some German musical terms in your part that you will expected to follow – or French and Italian terms. Your best bet is to buy a good pocket dictionary of musical terms and keep it in your gig bag. Over time, tempos markings such as *allegro* and *largo* will become second nature. But even after years of playing, you may run across terms you've never seen.

TIPS 75 – 86 : GIGGING

75 A GIG BY ANY OTHER NAME

Musicians refer to paying jobs – whether they're talking about weddings, pit orchestras, jazz clubs, or symphony orchestras – as gigs. Say the word a few times and use it with pride.

76 DRESSING FOR SUCCESS

What to wear for an audition or a gig takes a little more thought than dressing for a party or a day at the office. First, you have to know what attire is appropriate and expected. If you are playing an audition, you want to look competent and professional. If you are playing a recital, you will to wear something dressier. If you are soloing with ensemble, such as an orchestra or a band, you may need tails if you're a man, or a long gown if you're a woman. If you are playing in an orchestra or band, you may be asked to wear concert black, which means that arms and legs are covered in black. Women should note that black lace is usually not allowed, as it looks like patterned fabric to the audience. You may also be asked to wear black and white, which means a white blouse and a black, floor-length skirt or slacks for women, and black tux pants and a white dinner jacket for men. Always ask what attire is required or expected for a gig. Never assume.

Practice in your gig clothes. Make sure you can move your arms freely and can breathe deeply. If you have to stand as you play, make sure you can play comfortably in the shoes you plan to wear. Women take note: teetering and wobbling on high heels does nothing good for your sound. Women should also think about necklines and how much they will expose when it comes time to take a bow.

No matter what gig you're playing, keep the word "respect" in mind. Dress with respect for the ensemble in which you're playing, for the composer(s) whose music you're playing, and for the audience.

77 DEALING WITH NERVES

All musicians experience stage fright at some point in their careers. You can help diminish the external symptoms of nerves – trembling hands, shallow, rapid breathing, perspiration, and so on – simply by limiting the amount of caffeine and sugar you consume in the hours before you play. Many musicians cut out caffeine completely for several weeks before an audition or an important performance.

In addition to cutting out foods that can cause the same symptoms as nervousness, make sure you get plenty of sleep in the days leading up to an audition or performance. Lack of sleep can also cause or enhance physical symptoms of nervousness.

Preparation is the best cure for nerves. Prepare yourself well for the performance, which of course means plenty of practice and rehearsal, and then trust yourself. The more you get out there and perform, the more you trust yourself to do well and the less you will fight nerves.

Setting up a couple of mock performances, which means playing through your entire audition or concert program in front of an audience of family and friends, can help dampen nerves when the big day arrives.

78 THE WINDS OF CHANGE

Just as e-readers, such as the Kindle and the Nook, are changing the way many people read books, tablets designed for musicians are beginning to change the way some musicians read their music. Some of the digital music readers are built into music stands and some have a foot pedal to "turn pages" on the device. They are designed so that the individual musician can make marks in the music, just as they would in pencil on paper music.

You don't need to run out and buy yourself a digital music reader, but you can expect to see more of these in the future. It would be a good idea to keep an eye on them and make sure you at least know the basics of using one.

79 ON TIME IS LATE

"If you're not early, you're late," was some of the best gigging advice I ever received.

"Call time" is the time the contractor (the person who hired you) tells you to show up for a gig. That's the time at which the contractor takes roll call and starts making phone calls if people are not present. Always get to the gig before call time. You want to be set up, warmed up, relaxed, and ready to play at call time rather than racing through door shouting, "I'm here!" If you're caught in traffic, have an accident or some other unforeseeable delay, call the contractor immediately to let him or her know you're running late and when you will arrive, or worse, that you won't be arriving at all. This may seem like an obvious statement, but don't leave home for the gig without the contractor's phone number.

If the contractor sees you warming up 15 minutes before call time, dressed appropriately for the rehearsal or gig, you will not get a second thought. But if the contractor is looking at his or her watch wondering where you are or worse, waiting at the door when you arrive, you have blown it. The contractor will remember the stress of not knowing if you would show up and will probably think twice before hiring you again.

80 GEAR UP

If you spend some time talking to working musicians, you'll begin to hear stories of forgotten items, such as someone who had to fashion a bow tie out of black electrician's tape before going onstage because he left his at home. Or perhaps the one about someone borrowing a can of black spray paint from a stagehand to turn a pair of white socks into black socks. Not so funny are the stories of someone showing up for a gig without music, a mouthpiece, reeds, or any number of other essential items.

To avoid being the source of an often-repeated story, keep a gig checklist. The list should include every item you may need, from whatever attire is required – including shoes, socks, necktie, etc. – to a pencil, music stand, flute/piccolo stand, light, piccolo, stand clips (for holding music in place when playing outside), eyeglasses, sunglasses (for an outdoor gig), and so on.

Keep the list handy and refer to it before you leave the house for any gig or rehearsal. Never assume the items on the list are in your gig bag – always check to make sure they're there.

81 THE BIG OOPS

It may sound like a silly bit of paranoia, but while you're checking to make sure all the items on your gig checklist are in your bag, take a moment and open your case – or cases, if you're taking several instruments – to make sure that the instrument is actually there.

It's entirely possible to take the head joint of your flute out of the case to clean it and then forget to put it back. The few seconds it takes to open your case and check on its contents can save you from an embarrassing situation.

 82 WET YOUR WHISTLE

You've undoubtedly noticed that you're thirsty by the end of a practice session, lesson, rehearsal, or gig. Flutists use a tremendous amount of air, which dries out the delicate tissues of the mouth and throat as they play. Keeping a bottle of fresh water in your gig bag is a good insurance policy against finding your lips too dry to create a clean, focused sound or developing an annoying tickle in the throat from dryness.

Keep that water bottle clean. Washing it regularly with hot, soapy water will keep bacteria from building up and that, in turn, will help keep you healthy and keep the water tasting good.

 83 TECHNO NO-NO

Turn off your phone. When you get to rehearsal, turn off your phone. When you get to a gig, turn off your phone. When you sit down to listen to a performance, turn off your phone. When you sit down for a jam session, turn off your phone. When you begin a flute lesson, turn off your phone. When you sit down to practice, turn off your phone. Don't just silence it; turn it off. The buzz many phones make while silenced is quite audible. Don't check or send emails and texts while on a gig. You may think no one will notice, but the light coming off of your phone's screen is like a beacon. People will notice. Just turn off your phone. While you're at it, turn off your pager, your tablet, and any other bits of technology you may have brought along.

84 AT FIRST SIGHT?

Every now and then you will be called upon to sight-read, or play music you've never seen before, at a gig or in a rehearsal. This means you will be given a piece of music and asked to perform it on the spot. Changes in a concert program and last minute calls from a contractor are two of the most common reasons for being asked to sight-read in a work situation. Your willingness to take the gig and to sight-read will be appreciated. In these situations, everyone knows you're sight-reading and is pulling for you to do well. Everyone around you may be sight-reading as well.

Some of your best preparation for sight-reading on a gig can be done on a daily basis. The more you sight-read, the easier it gets. Start with simple, straightforward pieces. set a metronome and play. As you get more comfortable sight-reading, ramp up the difficulty level just a bit.

85 THE DEVIL'S IN THE DETAILS

Whenever you sight-read a piece or, for that matter, whenever you play any piece of music, make certain you know what you're doing before you make a single sound. Check the time signature, key signature, tempo marking, and dynamic marking before you dive in. As you play, keep your eyes slightly ahead of the notes you're actually playing to avoid surprises. Pay attention to all the ink on the page, which includes dynamic markings, repeats, etc.

It's more important to keep on playing and stay with the group than it is to play every note on the page. When sight-reading fast runs, it's better to play just the notes in the run that fall on the beats than to shoot for every note and slow down or lose your place in the process. Ornaments such as trills and turns can be omitted when you're sight-reading on the job.

86 EMERGENCY! EMERGENCY!

No matter how careful you are with your instrument, there will still come a day when you are on the road or at a gig and will have to make some minor repair to get through the day. Remembering that repairs are best performed by a qualified repair person, there are still some quick fixes you should be prepared to do. You should always carry an emergency repair kit for these situations. It's a good idea to take an emergency repair class if you see one offered in your area, or spend a little time watching your flute repair person work, if he or she will allow it. Failing that, there are some online videos that detail basic emergency flute repairs that may help you.

Your emergency repair kit should contain:

- A set of small screwdrivers that fit the adjusting screws on your flute.

- A spring pulling tool, or a small-gauge crochet hook, for popping springs back into place.

- A bottle of key oil with a fine nozzle, for getting a tiny bit of oil exactly where you might need it.

- A bottle of clear nail polish, for holding a loose screw in place once you have adjusted it.

- A pack of powdered papers or a key drying cloth (both available from music stores) for fixing sticky keys.

- Some small sheets of adhesive-backed cork in several thicknesses, for replacing corks that may drop off your flute.

- A single-edged razor blade for cutting the cork.

- Tweezers, for slipping the replacement cork in place.

- A handful of replacement pads and shims, in case one of your pads is damaged.

- A book of matches or a lighter, for melting the glue on the replacement pads.

Remember, some of these items will not be allowed in your carry-on luggage when flying. Be certain you know what you can and cannot take in the passenger cabin of a plane and stow those items in your checked baggage to avoid having them confiscated at the airport.

87 *TAKE CARE OF YOURSELF*

Your lips, lungs, hands, and arms are as much a part of your instrument as the keys on your flute. You have to take good care of them in order to play your best.

Lips

If your lips are chapped or sunburned, you'll struggle to control your sound. Keep lip balm handy at all times – preferably one that includes a sun-blocking agent – and apply it after you're done playing and whenever you go out in the wind and sun. Applying lip balm before you go to sleep can also help keep your lips from chapping. Be sure to remove it before playing, or it will create a sticky film inside your flute and on the pads.

When you have to go out in very cold weather, wear a muffler or scarf large enough to pull up over your lips and lower face. Just as your hands and feet get stiff and sluggish when they're cold, so do your lips.

Avoid salty foods. Salt can make your lips and the delicate tissue in your mouth retain water and swell, which makes it difficult to control your sound as you play.

Lungs

Don't smoke. Just don't.

Be aware of air quality. Dust and particulate matter in the air can cause irritation and coughing for quite a while after you're exposed to it. Always remember to wear a protective mask when sanding, sawing, or doing anything else that might create excessive dust.

Cold air can be rough on the lungs. That same muffler or scarf you draw up over your mouth to protect your lips will also protect your lungs from blasts of excessively cold air that can trigger bouts coughing or asthma attacks in those prone to asthma.

Hands

Your hands need to be relaxed and warm for you to play your best. Always wear mittens or gloves in cold weather. Be careful of odd non-musical tasks, such as wringing out clothing while doing hand washing, kneading bread, chopping wood, etc. Anything that makes your hands stiff and sore will have a negative impact on your playing.

A bandage on a fingertip takes away your ability to feel the key beneath your finger. If you're playing an open hole flute, it also keeps you from sealing the open hole. Keep a set of key plugs in your case in the event you have to play with a bandaged finger. Bear in mind that key plugs are not universal in size. Make sure the plugs you purchase will actually fit your flute.

Arms

Most of the same advice for keeping your hands in good playing shape applies to your arms as well. Warm, relaxed arms are essential to having warm, relaxed hands and to playing well. Just wearing long sleeves and keeping a sweater handy can make all the difference. Don't overdo exercise or activity that can make you arms tired, stiff, and sore.

88 MIRROR, MIRROR...

The reason dancers work in front mirrors on a daily basis is that they can't see themselves dance. They have to polish their every move and stance in front of mirrors, memorizing the physical feel of those moves and stances so they can reproduce them consistently when they're not in front of a mirror.

Playing the flute is similar, in that you can't see your hands, posture, or embouchure while you're playing. Borrowing the mirror idea from dancers, practice in front of a mirror periodically, to keep tabs on smooth, minimal finger motion, angles of wrists and elbows, and posture. A mirror can also help when learning new embouchure techniques.

89 INJURIES

No matter how careful you are about staying warm and relaxed as you play, you may experience a playing-related injury at some point in your playing career. Pay attention to any aches or pains you might feel as you play. Talk to your teacher about them. If they persist, don't hesitate to see a music medicine specialist. And yes, there is an entire field of medicine devoted not just to treating the playing-related injuries of musicians, but preventing those injuries in the first place.

90 FASTER FINGERS

If you are getting a little tired of the fast fingers exercise that makes use of the first five notes of each of your major scales, try the same warm-up using the first five notes of your minor scales. Looking at a sheet of minor scales, simply move from one to the next, playing the warm-up pattern you already know.

TRACK 21

Fast fingers (♩ = 80)

You may also do this exercise using your chromatic scale. Turn to the chromatic scale in this book (page 22). Start on any note you like and play five notes (ascending and descending in the pattern you already know) of your chromatic scale. Move either up or down by one half-step and play the first five notes of that chromatic scale. Keep moving in that direction until you land on the note an octave away from where you started.

TRACK 22

Fast fingers (♩ = 80)

91 WHAT A TRILL!

Flutists do a lot of trilling. Get used to it. Trills are indicated by the abbreviation *tr* and sometimes by the by ᵕᵕ. Either one of these symbols will be placed above the note to be trilled. Trilling is simply moving back and forth from the written note to the note above it in the key signature, quickly and smoothly, for the duration of the printed note.

TRACK 23

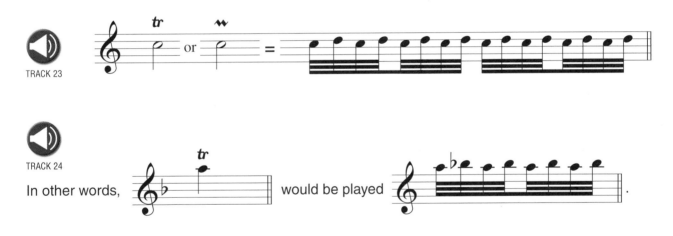

TRACK 24

In other words,   would be played

If the note to which you're trilling is different that the key signature indicates, the composer will place a sharp or flat beside the still symbol.

TRACK 25

When you come to trills in your music, make an exercise of them, practicing them slowly to secure the trill fingering and moving gradually into quicker tempos.

92 ON THE DOUBLE – OR TRIPLE!

The day is going to come when you hit a passage in a piece of music that is simply moving too quickly for you to tongue it as it's marked. The solution for this situation is found in double tonguing. Double tonguing is just a matter of building on single tonguing – so you're halfway there already. To double tongue, you alternate the "too" sound you've been making to articulate notes with a "koo" sound, made further back in mouth than the "too." It feels a bit like your tongue is rocking from front to back as you double tongue.

As with any new technique on the flute, start out slowly and speed it up gradually. Remember that a strong, steady stream of air is just as important as steady, even use of the tongue when you are double tonguing. Use a major scale for your double tonguing practice and warm up as follows:

TRACK 26

Moderately fast (♩ = 132)

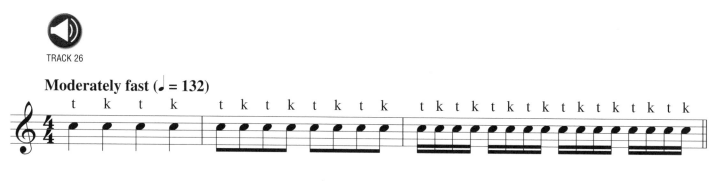

93 TRIPLE PLAY

Think for a minute about double tonguing triplets. Confused? Don't worry, there's a solution. Just as we added a "koo" sound to single tonguing to create double tonguing, we are going to add a "too" sound to double tonguing to create triple tonguing. You'll be tonguing on the syllables T-K-T, T-K-T. Steady air and even tonguing are equally important in clean triple tonguing. The following exercise/ warm-up should help you get going on your triple tonguing.

TRACK 27

Moderately fast (♩ = 132)

94 VIBRATO

Listen to your favorite singer and you will almost undoubtedly notice a shimmer, or gentle pulse, within that singer's sound that adds depth and color the music. That shimmer is called vibrato and is one of the expressive tools at your disposal as a flutist. The sound is created within the air stream, so there's no external movement to think about or coordinate.

Step one in learning to use vibrato is listening to vibrato in others. You'll hear it in the sound of singers, string players, and most woodwind players. By tradition, most clarinetists use vibrato very rarely, if at all. Brass players use vibrato in some genres of music and rarely in others. You may hear a trumpeter using vibrato in an expressive jazz solo, but not in the chorale passages of a symphony.

Listen to the way vibrato stays within a musician's sound. It never chops the sound into little bursts. Listen to way some musicians alter the speed of their vibrato. A fast, shallow vibrato adds an energy or urgency to the sound, while a slower, wider vibrato adds warmth and color.

Many teachers will tell you that vibrato will appear on its own, as a natural part of a well-supported sound. Some teachers will help you jump-start your vibrato by recommending some version of the following vibrato exercise.

Starting on your third octave D, play a long tone with a big, strong sound. Repeat the note, making slow, strong pulses in your air stream, speeding them up gradually. Do this as part of your warm-up for a couple of days and then work on speeding up the pulses a bit. After a few days, speed them up again, continuing this process until you are comfortable with the feel and process of adding a rhythmic pulse to your sound. You may now begin adding vibrato to longer notes in a simple melody. Remember that vibrato in fast passages just sounds like nervous clutter. Vibrato is an ornament, not a constant fixture in your sound. Use it expressively.

TRACK 28

Flutists of the 20th and 21st centuries have a technical challenge that their predecessors never faced: extended techniques. Some "new music" asks for effects from flutists, in addition to traditional playing. Some music will give great detail on how the flutist is to create the desired effect, for instance instructing the player to remove the head joint, bring the barrel of the instrument to his or her mouth and then buzz as though playing a trumpet, while fingering specific notes. Try it – it's a pretty curious sound.

Other composers will instruct the flutist to perform more standard extended techniques, such as flutter tonguing, pitch bending (fall offs), and harmonics. These are not things that come up often in one's playing, so don't worry about mastering a new set of flute skills all at once. Flutists tend to learn these techniques one at a time, when a piece requires it of them.

Flutter tonguing is a matter of creating a rolled or burred "r" sound inside your mouth as you play. Practice saying a few words with a strong rolled r, such as rrrain or rrready). Play a third octave D on your flute and try adding the rolled or burred sound to the note. Keep your air stream steady and prepare yourself for a harsher sound than you're accustomed to making. Most composers use little strips on the stems to indicate flutter tonguing (Flatterzunge in German). Others write "flz" in the score.

TRACK 29

Pitch bending is a simple matter of raising or lowering your head to alter the pitch of a single note. It's just an exaggerated version of what you do while determining if you're sharp or flat as you tune. Do not roll the flute, as this interferes with hand position and is difficult to control. Raising your head raises the pitch of the note and lowering your head lowers the pitch. If you go too far in either direction, you will cut off the sound.

TRACK 30

Harmonics are thin, almost ghostly, versions of notes. They require steady air and a focused embouchure. Play a low D Add a little air and you will move an octave higher. Add a little more air and you will move to a A Add yet more and focus and you can move up to a rather hollow-sounding high D. It does not sound like the standard fingering for the D and that's the point. This is an effect that is used infrequently.

Harmonics are indicated as followed:

TRACK 31

96 EXTENDED RANGE

Although flute fingering charts take you up to high C and call that the end of the flute's range, a fair amount of music written in the 20th century asks you venture well above that note. The flute's fourth octave, any note above high C, is strange territory. You are playing notes that are outside the range the flute was designed to cover.

As a result, there is not a single set of fingerings that will work on all flutes, but there are lots of options. Some fingerings work on some flutes, but not others. Sometimes several fingerings will work for a single note, in which case the players should choose the one that is easiest to use in the context of the music. In order to play a fourth octave D, for instance, you have to find a list of possible fingerings and try them on your flute.

Until fairly recently, fourth octave fingerings were passed from teachers to students and guarded carefully, because most of the fingerings weren't in print anywhere. Now, you can do an Internet search for "flute fourth octave fingerings" and come up with more hits than you will want to view. The first few should provide all the information you need.

Like extended techniques, most flutists learn the extended range notes one at a time, when a piece requires it of them.

97 EXTENDING THE EXTENDED TECHNIQUES

A few more extended techniques you may run across include the jet whistle, whistle tones, and key slaps.

The **jet whistle**, most famously used in Heitor Villa-Lobos's "Assobio a Jato" (The Jet Whistle), is a shrieking sound made by covering the entire lip plate with your mouth and blowing extremely forcefully into the flute. Changing fingerings and changing the angle of your mouth on the lip plate will alter the sound of the jet whistle. Be careful to practice this effect in small doses – it's very easy to find yourself lightheaded while working on this effect.

Jet whistles are indicated as follows:

TRACK 32

Whistle tones are completely unrelated to the jet whistle, but they are related to harmonics. They are thin, ghostly sounds created by working gently up the harmonic series from a base tone.

Finger high F and blow an extremely gentle, thin stream of air. Listen closely and adjust the air until you hear a faint whistle. Whistle tones are easiest in this register. The more you can control whistle tones, the more you will be able to control your soft dynamics.

Whistle tones are indicated as follows:

TRACK 33

Key slaps, which are sometimes called key clicks or key percussion, are produced by slapping down the keys of the flute with no air moving through the instrument. The body of the flute creates a resonating chamber that amplifies the slap. Finger low D and slap the G key several times. Remember: no air should be moving through the flute.

Key slaps are indicated as follows:

TRACK 34

TIPS ❾❽ – ❶❶❶: READY, SET, GO!

❾❽ TIME TO PLAY

Practicing has to be a solitary, focused experience, but playing an instrument is about more than just practicing. Get out and play! Look for groups or situations in your area that offer opportunities to play. Many areas have community orchestras or bands; some have groups that rehearse and perform during the summer only. Many places of worship welcome performers for services and for special events. Many urban areas have a flute club or flute choir that gives occasional performances.

Music stores and music teachers are a good source of information on local playing opportunities. Another good source is listings of community events in newspapers, on television, on the radio, or the Internet. You can also do a search on any one of the popular web search engines. Enter the name of your city or town and "community band" or "community orchestra." You may be surprised by the number of groups in your area.

99 SWITCHEROO

Sometimes a change of pace is all you need to spark your drive to practice. Try picking up a related instrument, perhaps the Irish tin whistle, and work on a few tunes and the Celtic style of playing and ornamenting. The fingerings are nearly identical to the flute – and playing the little instrument can be musically liberating.

Recorders can also offer some variety. Like the flute, they can be purchased in several different keys and ranges. Native American flutes, also available in several keys and pitch ranges, as well as ethnic flutes from around the world, can be a lot of fun to play. They can inspire you to listen to and learn about the music of other cultures.

If you have a hankering to play some Revolutionary War tunes, try a fife. Blown like a flute – or, more accurately, like a piccolo – a fife is actually a keyless version of the latter.

Although tin whistles are also known as penny whistles, the days of getting one for a penny are gone. They are still a great bargain, at $10 to $15. Plastic recorders start at about $7 and plastic fifes start at about $14.

100 FLUTE FRATERNIZATION

Joining an orchestra, band, or chamber group is an essential part of developing as a musician. Joining a flute ensemble or flute club can be a real help in developing as a flutist. It also gives you a community of like-minded colleagues that can be a big help in finding a teacher, finding the best local deals on instruments and music, and in finding a group of friends who enjoy the same concerts and events you do.

Joining the National Flute Association is a good way to keep on top of what's going on in the flute world. The N.F.A.'s annual convention, which is in a different city each year, is a great venue for hearing a lot of fine flutists and for checking the latest recordings, music, and accessories for the instrument.

Don't forget to check the Internet. There are a lot of flute pages, forums, and chat rooms that you may find interesting.

101 ENJOY!

It would be almost criminal to offer 101 tips on flute playing without reminding you to enjoy yourself. Therefore, Tip #101 is just that: Enjoy yourself! Whether you are practicing or performing, taking a lesson, listening to a performance, or reading about your favorite style of music, remember how fortunate you are to have this outlet in your life. Enjoy every moment of it.

By the way, the answer to the question you will be asked again and again as people learn that you play the flute is a simple one: "Either flutist or flautist is correct."

HAL•LEONARD INSTRUMENTAL PLAY-ALONG

Your favorite songs are arranged just for solo instrumentalists with this outstanding series. Each book includes a great full-accompaniment play-along CD so you can sound just like a pro! Check out **www.halleonard.com** to see all the titles available.

Disney Greats

Arabian Nights • Hawaiian Roller Coaster Ride • It's a Small World • Look Through My Eyes • Yo Ho (A Pirate's Life for Me) • and more.

_____	00841934	Flute	$12.95
_____	00841935	Clarinet	$12.95
_____	00841936	Alto Sax	$12.95
_____	00841937	Tenor Sax	$12.95
_____	00841938	Trumpet	$12.95
_____	00841939	Horn	$12.95
_____	00841940	Trombone	$12.95
_____	00841941	Violin	$12.95
_____	00841942	Viola	$12.95
_____	00841943	Cello	$12.95
_____	00842078	Oboe	$12.95

Glee

And I Am Telling You I'm Not Going • Defying Gravity • Don't Stop Believin' • Keep Holding On • Lean on Me • No Air • Sweet Caroline • True Colors • and more.

_____	00842479	Flute	$12.99
_____	00842480	Clarinet	$12.99
_____	00842481	Alto Sax	$12.99
_____	00842482	Tenor Sax	$12.99
_____	00842483	Trumpet	$12.99
_____	00842484	Horn	$12.99
_____	00842485	Trombone	$12.99
_____	00842486	Violin	$12.99
_____	00842487	Viola	$12.99
_____	00842488	Cello	$12.99

Motown Classics

ABC • Endless Love • I Just Called to Say I Love You • My Girl • The Tracks of My Tears • What's Going On • You've Really Got a Hold on Me • and more.

_____	00842572	Flute	$12.99
_____	00842573	Clarinet	$12.99
_____	00842574	Alto Saxophone	$12.99
_____	00842575	Tenor Saxophone	$12.99
_____	00842576	Trumpet	$12.99
_____	00842577	Horn	$12.99
_____	00842578	Trombone	$12.99
_____	00842579	Violin	$12.99
_____	00842580	Viola	$12.99
_____	00842581	Cello	$12.99

Popular Hits

Breakeven • Fireflies • Halo • Hey, Soul Sister • I Gotta Feeling • I'm Yours • Need You Now • Poker Face • Viva La Vida • You Belong with Me • and more.

_____	00842511	Flute	$12.99
_____	00842512	Clarinet	$12.99
_____	00842513	Alto Sax	$12.99
_____	00842514	Tenor Sax	$12.99
_____	00842515	Trumpet	$12.99
_____	00842516	Horn	$12.99
_____	00842517	Trombone	$12.99
_____	00842518	Violin	$12.99
_____	00842519	Viola	$12.99
_____	00842520	Cello	$12.99

Sports Rock

Another One Bites the Dust • Centerfold • Crazy Train • Get Down Tonight • Let's Get It Started • Shout • The Way You Move • and more.

_____	00842326	Flute	$12.99
_____	00842327	Clarinet	$12.99
_____	00842328	Alto Sax	$12.99
_____	00842329	Tenor Sax	$12.99
_____	00842330	Trumpet	$12.99
_____	00842331	Horn	$12.99
_____	00842332	Trombone	$12.99
_____	00842333	Violin	$12.99
_____	00842334	Viola	$12.99
_____	00842335	Cello	$12.99

Women of Pop

Bad Romance • Jar of Hearts • Mean • My Life Would Suck Without You • Our Song • Rolling in the Deep • Single Ladies (Put a Ring on It) • Teenage Dream • and more.

_____	00842650	Flute	$12.99
_____	00842651	Clarinet	$12.99
_____	00842652	Alto Sax	$12.99
_____	00842653	Tenor Sax	$12.99
_____	00842654	Trumpet	$12.99
_____	00842655	Horn	$12.99
_____	00842656	Trombone	$12.99
_____	00842657	Violin	$12.99
_____	00842658	Viola	$12.99
_____	00842659	Cello	$12.99

Twilight

Bella's Lullaby • Decode • Eyes on Fire • Full Moon • Go All the Way (Into the Twilight) • Leave Out All the Rest • Spotlight (Twilight Remix) • Supermassive Black Hole • Tremble for My Beloved.

_____	00842406	Flute	$12.99
_____	00842407	Clarinet	$12.99
_____	00842408	Alto Sax	$12.99
_____	00842409	Tenor Sax	$12.99
_____	00842410	Trumpet	$12.99
_____	00842411	Horn	$12.99
_____	00842412	Trombone	$12.99
_____	00842413	Violin	$12.99
_____	00842414	Viola	$12.99
_____	00842415	Cello	$12.99

Twilight – New Moon

Almost a Kiss • Dreamcatcher • Edward Leaves • I Need You • Memories of Edward • New Moon • Possibility • Roslyn • Satellite Heart • and more.

_____	00842458	Flute	$12.99
_____	00842459	Clarinet	$12.99
_____	00842460	Alto Sax	$12.99
_____	00842461	Tenor Sax	$12.99
_____	00842462	Trumpet	$12.99
_____	00842463	Horn	$12.99
_____	00842464	Trombone	$12.99
_____	00842465	Violin	$12.99
_____	00842466	Viola	$12.99
_____	00842467	Cello	$12.99

Wicked

As Long As You're Mine • Dancing Through Life • Defying Gravity • For Good • I'm Not That Girl • Popular • The Wizard and I • and more.

_____	00842236	Book/CD Pack	$11.95
_____	00842237	Book/CD Pack	$11.95
_____	00842238	Alto Saxophone	$11.95
_____	00842239	Tenor Saxophone	$11.95
_____	00842240	Trumpet	$11.95
_____	00842241	Horn	$11.95
_____	00842242	Trombone	$11.95
_____	00842243	Violin	$11.95
_____	00842244	Viola	$11.95
_____	00842245	Cello	$11.95

FOR MORE INFORMATION, SEE YOUR LOCAL MUSIC DEALER, OR WRITE TO:

HAL•LEONARD® CORPORATION

7777 W. BLUEMOUND RD. P.O. BOX 13819 MILWAUKEE, WI 53213